The Entrance Place of Wonders
POEMS OF THE HARLEM RENAISSANCE

selected by **Daphne Muse**

illustrated by **Charlotte Riley-Webb**

HARRY N. ABRAMS, INC., PUBLISHERS

Introduction

BY DAPHNE MUSE

There was a time when Harlem, New York, was the cultural center of the black world. Strong black men and women, who once bent over to pick cotton, arrived in Harlem standing tall. They came from the South—Alabama, South Carolina, Virginia, and Mississippi. They also came from islands in the Caribbean—Puerto Rico, Jamaica, Haiti, Nevis, Cuba, and Trinidad. Harlem grew into a community filled with the minds of great educators, artists, doctors, politicians, and some of the world's most memorable poets. While some of these poets were teachers and editors, others were active in organizations like the National Association for the Advancement of Colored People (NAACP) or Marcus Garvey's United Negro Improvement Association (UNIA). But all created time to write beautiful, bold, and sometimes painful black words.

A renaissance is a rebirth or revival, and in art, fiction, drama, and poetry, there was a lot to be reborn and revived. Centered in New York, this movement began in 1917, and voices emerged from Washington, D.C.; Chicago; and throughout the African diaspora. Harlem was alive with new life, ideas, and people. And, as black people planted new possibilities, they also grew big dreams. With its own symphony, record companies, theaters, and publishing houses, Harlem was a sprawling neighborhood at the northern end of New York City. This "mecca" was filled with magic, history, and culture. People came from all over the world to dance to great music, see fine art, and listen to exciting poets.

Many of the poems of the Harlem Renaissance were celebratory and life-affirming, changing the way black people thought about themselves and the world. While Harlem represented the heart of an urban environment, most of the poems chosen for *The Entrance Place of Wonders* invoke the pastoral—perhaps as an attempt to transcend the difficulties of city life through a return to the natural world.

While jazz and jive jumped up and down the streets, poems breezed out of windows. They also stepped out of doors. Some even pushed their way up out of the cracks in the sidewalks. If you listened carefully, you could hear poems pouring off the "A" train. But in 1929, the voices of some of these poets began to disappear because of the hardships of the Great Depression. It was a time when millions of people stood in soup lines to be fed. Jobs vanished. New to freedom, black people already understood what it was like to face hard times.

The last wave of the Harlem Renaissance washed ashore around 1935, leaving an unforgettable legacy. The poems of the Harlem Renaissance were remarkable—they changed black life and culture, and helped make this movement one of the most significant periods in American history. Through *The Entrance Place of Wonders,* the vibrant spirit of that amazing time lives on.

Biographical Information on the Featured Poets

Madeline G. Allison, Alpha Angela Bratton, and **Annette Browne** contributed poems to the *Brownies' Book*, a children's magazine founded in 1920 by the writer and foremost black intellectual of the twentieth century, W.E.B. DuBois. The magazine included poetry, folklore, fiction, photographs, current events, letters from young readers, and more.

William Stanley Braithwaite (1878–1962) was born in Boston, Massachusetts. As a self-educated man, he developed his love of poetry while serving as an apprentice to a printer. He served on the faculty of the English Department at Atlanta University and produced several award-winning volumes of poetry.

James Alpheus Butler, Jr. (dates unknown) graduated from the University of Denver and served as the editor of several literary journals, including the *Parnassian* and *Twentieth Century Review*. He was published in more than twenty-five volumes of poetry.

Carrie W. Clifford (1862–1934) was born in Chillicothe, Ohio, and became a civil rights activist. The themes in her poetry include injustice, slavery, democracy, and race. She also opened up her Washington, D.C., home as a literary salon where black intellectuals gathered.

Countee Cullen (1903–1946) was born in Louisville, Kentucky. As a high school student in New York City, he won a citywide poetry contest for one of his first poems, "I Have a Rendezvous with Life." He received an M.A. from Harvard University, taught French, and wrote several clever books of poetry for children, including *The Lost Zoo* and *Christopher Cat*.

Gladys May Caseley-Hayford (Aquah LaLuah) (1904–1950) was born in Axim on the African Gold Coast (Ghana), and attended Penrohs College in Wales. She often wrote of her deep love and appreciation for the beauty of Africa and her people.

Langston Hughes (1902–1967) was born in Joplin, Missouri, and took his bow into the world of literature as class poet in the eighth grade. He wrote several books for children, often incorporating folk and jazz rhythms into his work. From Africa to Europe, and all across America, his beloved poetry is read and studied.

Jessie Redmon Fauset (1882–1961) was born in Fredericksville, New Jersey, and was considered a mentor and "midwife" of the Renaissance. She taught Latin and French in Washington, D.C., and was both the literary and managing editor of the *Brownies' Book*.

Dorothy Vena Johnson (1898–1970) was born in Los Angeles, California, and taught creative writing in the public school system. *Nuggets,* an early-twentieth-century poetry magazine by and for children, carried contributions from several of her students. Her work has appeared in numerous anthologies of the period.

Georgia Douglas Johnson (1880–1966) was born in Atlanta, Georgia, and became a teacher and prolific writer. Her career as a poet blossomed as a result of her admiration for the poems of William Stanley Braithwaite. Her home in Washington, D.C., was an important meeting place for writers and artists.

James Weldon Johnson (1871–1938) was born in Jacksonville, Florida, and served as a high-school principal and member of the diplomatic corps before becoming a poet. He composed "Lift Every Voice and Sing," the Negro National Anthem, and his poetry is included in many major literary anthologies in America and around the world.

Claude McKay (1889–1948) was born in Clarendon, Jamaica, West Indies, and came to the U.S. to study. At age twenty, he published his first book of poetry. His widely read work was an inspiration for many other writers of the Harlem Renaissance, such as Langston Hughes.

Effie Lee Newsome (1885–1979) was born in Philadelphia, Pennsylvania, and served as a librarian at Central State College and Wilberforce University in Ohio. In 1940, her collection *Gladiola Garden: Poems of Outdoors and Indoors for Second Grade Readers* was published.

The Wishing Game

BY ANNETTE BROWNE

We gathered 'round the fire last night,
Jim an' Bess an' me,
And said, "Now let us each in turn
Tell who we'd rather be,
Of all the folks that's in our books."
(Of course, we wouldn't want their looks.)

Bess wished that she'd been Betsy Ross,
The first to make the flag.
She said, "I'd like to do some deed
To make the people brag,
And have the papers print my name—
If colored girls could rise to fame."

An' I stood out for Roosevelt;
I wished to be like him.
Then Bess said, "We've both had our say,
Now tell who you'd be, Jim."
Jim never thinks like me or Bess,
He knows more than us both, I guess.

He said, "I'd be a Paul Dunbar
Or Booker Washington.
The folks you named were good, I know.
But you see, Tom, each one
Of these two men I'd wish to be
Were colored boys, like you and me.

Sojourner Truth was colored, Bess,
And Phillis Wheatley, too;
Their names will live like Betsy Ross,
Though they were dark like you."
Jim's read of 'em somewhere, I guess,
He knows heaps more than me or Bess.

Tableau

BY COUNTEE CULLEN

Locked arm in arm they cross the way,
   The black boy and the white,
The golden splendor of the day,
   The sable pride of night.

From lowered blinds the dark folk stare,
   And here the fair folk talk,
Indignant that these two should dare
   In unison to walk.

Oblivious to look and word
   They pass, and see no wonder
That lightning brilliant as a sword
   Should blaze the path of thunder.

To You

BY LANGSTON HUGHES

To sit and dream, to sit and read,
To sit and learn about the world
Outside our world of here and now—
    our problem world—
To dream of vast horizons of the soul
Through dreams made whole,
Unfettered free—help me!
All you who are dreamers, too,
Help me make our world anew.
I reach out my hands to you.

Sassafras Tea

BY EFFIE LEE NEWSOME

The sassafras tea is red and clear
   In my white china cup,
So pretty I keep peeping in
   Before I drink it up.

      I stir it with a silver spoon,
         And sometimes I just hold
      A little tea inside the spoon,
         Like it was lined with gold.

            It makes me hungry just to smell
               The nice hot sassafras tea,
            And that's one thing I really like
              That they say's good for me.

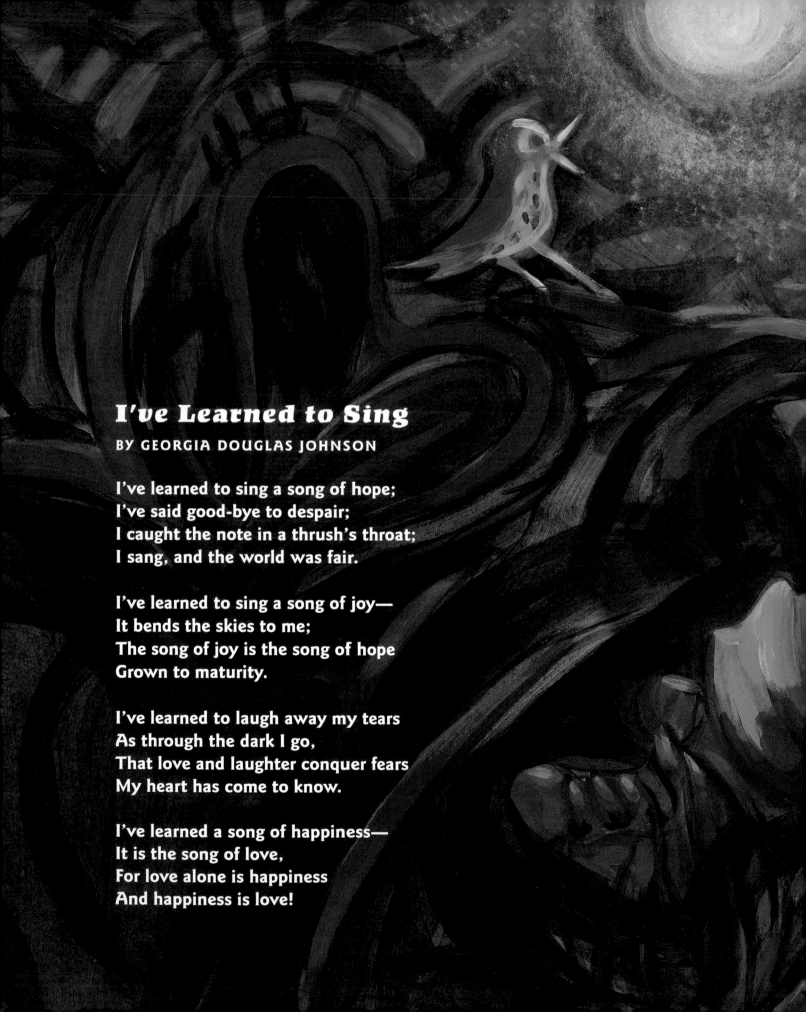

I've Learned to Sing

BY GEORGIA DOUGLAS JOHNSON

I've learned to sing a song of hope;
I've said good-bye to despair;
I caught the note in a thrush's throat;
I sang, and the world was fair.

I've learned to sing a song of joy—
It bends the skies to me;
The song of joy is the song of hope
Grown to maturity.

I've learned to laugh away my tears
As through the dark I go,
That love and laughter conquer fears
My heart has come to know.

I've learned a song of happiness—
It is the song of love,
For love alone is happiness
And happiness is love!

The Gift to Sing

BY JAMES WELDON JOHNSON

Sometimes the mist overhangs my path,
And blackening clouds about me cling;
But, oh, I have a magic way
To turn the gloom to cheerful day—
    I softly sing.

And if the way grows darker still,
Shadowed by Sorrow's somber wing,
With glad defiance in my throat,
I pierce the darkness with a note,
    And sing, and sing.

I brood not over the broken past,
Nor dread whatever time may bring;
No nights are dark, no days are long,
While in my heart there swells a song,
    And I can sing.

Your World

BY GEORGIA DOUGLAS JOHNSON

Your world is as big as you make it.
I know, for I used to abide
In the narrowest nest in a corner,
My wings pressing close to my side.

But I sighted the distant horizon
Where the skyline encircled the sea
And I throbbed with a burning desire
To travel this immensity.

I battered the cordons around me
And cradled my wings on the breeze,
Then soared to the uttermost reaches
With rapture, with power, with ease!

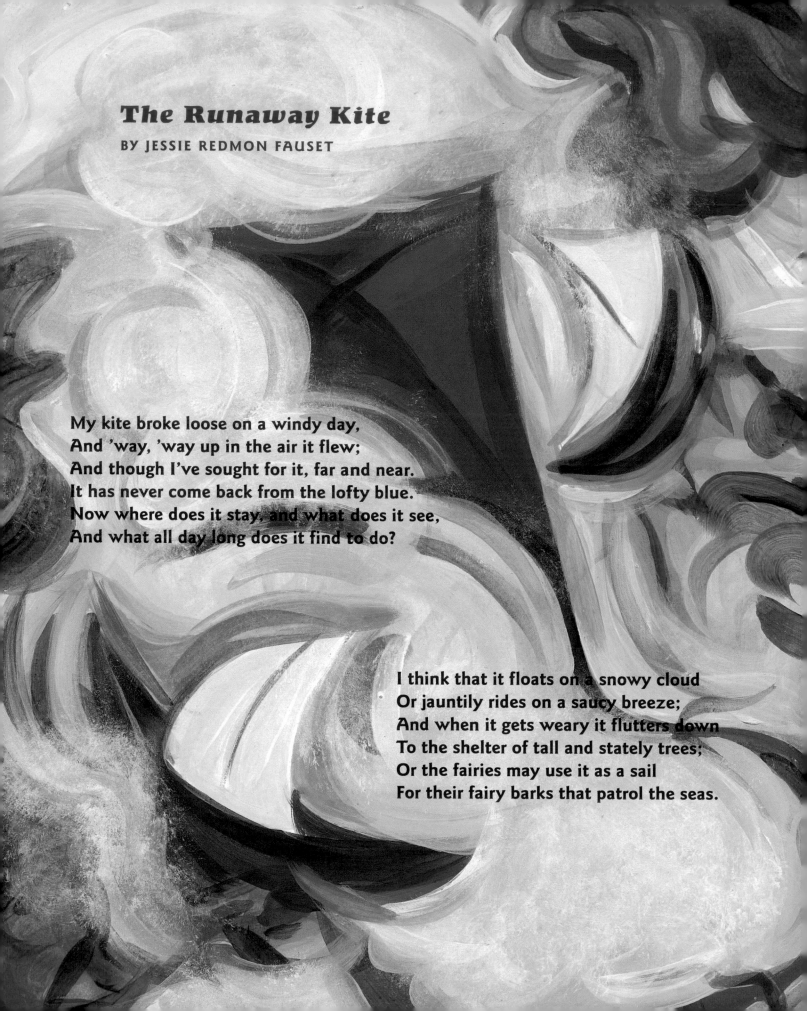

The Runaway Kite

BY JESSIE REDMON FAUSET

My kite broke loose on a windy day,
And 'way, 'way up in the air it flew;
And though I've sought for it, far and near.
It has never come back from the lofty blue.
Now where does it stay, and what does it see,
And what all day long does it find to do?

I think that it floats on a snowy cloud
Or jauntily rides on a saucy breeze;
And when it gets weary it flutters down
To the shelter of tall and stately trees;
Or the fairies may use it as a sail
For their fairy barks that patrol the seas.

Dream Variations

BY LANGSTON HUGHES

To fling my arms wide
In some place of the sun,
To whirl and to dance
Till the white day is done.
Then rest at cool evening
Beneath a tall tree
While night comes on gently,
    Dark like me—
That is my dream!

To fling my arms wide
In the face of the sun,
Dance! Whirl! Whirl!
Till the quick day is done.
Rest at pale evening . . .
A tall, slim tree . . .
Night coming tenderly
    Black like me.

Rhapsody

BY WILLIAM STANLEY BRAITHWAITE

I am glad daylong for the gift of song,
For time and change and sorrow;
For the sunset wings and the world-end things
Which hang on the edge of tomorrow.
I am glad for my heart whose gates apart
Are the entrance-place of wonders,
Where dreams come in from the rush and din
Like sheep from rains and thunders.

Palace

BY DOROTHY VENA JOHNSON

A SEA shell is a palace
Where many echoes dwell,
And when I listen to them
I know them all quite well.
They are like the ocean's roar
Where the sea shell buried deep
Learns why the sea is always salt,
And spooky shadows creep.

Slumber Song

BY ALPHA ANGELA BRATTON

Close those eyes where points of light
Shine like stars through the velvet night,
   Brownie Boy.
Lightly float in a dimpled smile
Out on the sea of "Dream-a-while."
With gold nets, dream-fish to beguile,
   Brownie Boy.

See how the big moon dips and swings,
Shaking the stars from its silver wings,
   Brownie Boy.
Come, let us follow, you and I.
Follow its flight across the sky.
Into the land of "Bye-and-Bye."
   Brownie Boy.

The changing years will come and go—
Summer's rose and winter's snow—
   Brownie Boy.
Stealing my brown boy from my breast;
Bringing him manhood's eager quest,
And splendid strength for every test,
   Brownie Boy.

Teaching you, too, from History's page,
The joy of your noble heritage,
   Brownie Boy.
Ah! You must needs be doubly true,
Doubly strong in the task you do.
Nor fail the Race that speaks in you,
   Brownie Boy.

Children of the Sun

BY MADELINE G. ALLISON

Dear little girl of tender years,
Born of a race with haunting fears—
Cry not nor sigh for wrongs done you,
Your cloud has silv'ry lining, too.

Dear little son, be not in gloom,
For fears this world has no more room;
God in his Wisdom gave you hue
Of which He's proud—yes, proud of you!

The Lizard

BY GLADYS MAY CASELEY-HAYFORD
(Aquah LaLuah)

I met a handsome lizard upon the gravel walk,
And so I stopped politely and asked him for
    a talk;
He nodded once, he nodded twice to make his
    meaning plain,
Glanced up at me with wee bright eyes and
    nodded once again.

I said, "You live on flies. Do you eat them
    alive or dead?
And when you eat them, do they still keep
    buzzing in your head?"
He shrugged, then very haughtily inclined to
    me his ear
Insinuating it was time I made my meaning
    clear.

"I'm sorry," I began, "but please, this
    question if I may;
Do you, Sir, shake your head for no and nod
    your head for aye?"
He glanced at me with cold disdain, ignoring
    me, until
He slowly and deliberately climbed on the
    windowsill
He turned, he nodded once, twice, thrice to
    make his meaning plain,
Glanced up at me, with wee bright eyes and
    nodded once again.

Winter Sweetness

BY LANGSTON HUGHES

This little house is sugar.
　　Its roof with snow is piled.
And from its tiny window,
　　Peeps a maple-sugar child.

A Kindergarten Song

BY CARRIE W. CLIFFORD

Little babies in a row,
Little dresses white as snow;
No hair, crinkled hair, straight hair, curls—
Lovely little boys and girls!

Little children in a ring,
Hear them as they gaily sing!
Red child, yellow child, black child, white—
That's what makes the ring all right.

Lad and lassie, youth and maid.
Born in sunshine, born in shade;
Zulu, Esquimaux, Saxon, Jew,
United, make the world come true!

God's big children all at work,
Not one dares his task to shirk;
"All for each, and each for all"—
White man, red man, black man, tall.

Common Things

BY JAMES ALPHEUS BUTLER, JR.

I LOVE to sit in forests green
'Mid tufts of grass in splendor seen,
And scent the flowers in the air,
And gaze with wond'ring, raptured stare
   On common things.

I love to haunt the woodland stream
Where water-lilies paint the scene,
Where meadow-sweet and water-cresses
Add color to the stream's recesses,
Where poppies red, in glory swaying,
Are with the yellow loose-stripes playing;
And then I pause, and think, and ponder,
And soon my heart is filled with wonder
   At common things.

I love to hear a passing bird
Trill notes the sweetest ever heard!
I love to hear the night-bird's screeches;
Or watch the squirrel in the beeches;
Each sight, each sound a new joy teaches
   In common things.

Spring in New Hampshire

BY CLAUDE MCKAY

Too green the springing April grass,
Too blue the silver-speckled sky,
For me to linger here, alas,
While happy winds go laughing by,
Wasting the golden hours indoors,
Washing windows and scrubbing floors.

Too wonderful the April night,
Too faintly sweet the first May flowers,
The stars too gloriously bright,
For me to spend the evening hours,
When fields are fresh and streams are leaping,
Wearied, exhausted, dully sleeping.

And This From Bruin Bear

BY COUNTEE CULLEN

As I must have honey
If I am to thrive,
Please see that you lodge me
Close to a hive.
I'll be ever so careful,
And try not to ruin
The tiniest Bee.
Yours faithfully: Bruin.

Next, From the Bees

BY COUNTEE CULLEN

DEAR NOAH: A rumor
Says we are to share
Our hive (and our honey!)
With Bruin the Bear!
We here go on record,
(We'd go on our knees
If Bees *had* knees)
As being opposed
To plans such as these.
Busily yours: the Bees.

To Arna Bontemps, the mentor who introduced me to the Harlem Renaissance in 1962, and
Louise Thompson Patterson—who lifted so many voices as the founder of Vanguard, a Harlem salon
—D.M.

To my grandchildren: Muffin, Courtney, Chris, Chloe, B2, Camille, Andrew, and Dylan
—C.R.W.

ARTIST'S NOTE
Having the opportunity to revisit and visually document the Harlem Renaissance was an honor for me. As a fine artist,
my current genre is abstract art, working in painting and pastels. For *The Entance Place of Wonders*,
I reincorporated my signature rhythmic style with bold colors and contemporary realism.
—C.R.W.

ACKNOWLEDGMENTS
Thanks to Tamar Brazis for being such a solid and supportive editor and
to the librarians whose invaluable assistance made this project possible.
—D.M.

"To You," "Dream Variations," and "Winter Sweetness" from *The Collected Poems of Langston Hughes* by
Langston Hughes, copyright © 1994 by the Estate of Langston Hughes. Used by permission of Alfred A. Knopf,
a division of Random House, Inc. Reprinted by permission of Harold Ober Associates Incorporated.

"The Gift to Sing," by James Weldon Johnson. Permission by Sondra Kathryn Wilson,
literary executor of the Estate of Grace and James Weldon Johnson.

"Tableau," "And This From Bruin Bear," and "Next, From the Bees" copyrights held by Amistad Research Center,
Tulane University, administered by Thompson and Thompson, New York, NY.

"Spring in New Hampshire" courtesy of the Literary Representative for the Works of Claude McKay, Schomburg Center for
Research in Black Culture, The New York Public Library, Astor, Lenox, and Tilden Foundations.

"The Wishing Game," "Slumber Song," "Children of the Sun," "A Kindergarten Song," and "Common Things" originally appeared in
The Brownies' Book, a magazine for children published by the NAACP from 1920–1921. Reprinted by permission of Oxford University Press.

A sustained and concerted effort was made to identify all copyright holders. The same effort was put into
fact-checking and verifying biographical information related to the poets whose works are featured in this collection.

Production Manager: Jonathan Lopes

Library of Congress Cataloging-in-Publication Data has been applied for.
ISBN 0-8109-5997-6

Printed and bound in China
10 9 8 7 6 5 4 3 2 1

Harry N. Abrams, Inc.
115 West 18th Street
New York, NY 10011
www.abramsbooks.com

Abrams is a subsidiary of

LA MARTINIÈRE
GROUPE

Children's Room